American Indian Tribal Hymns

American Indian Tribal Hymns

Tulsa Indian United Methodist Church

Oklafalaya Publishing

CONTENTS

CHAPTER vii
THE LORD'S PRAYER ix

1 | TRIBAL HYMNS 1

1901 NORTH COLLEGE AVENUE

(918) 834-1956

Original developed October 23, 1989

Second developed February 11, 2023

MISSION STATEMENT

We, the members of Tulsa Indian United Methodist Church are committed to worshipping God, growing in faith, and ministering to the physical, emotional, and spiritual needs of the community.

Ubanumpa Chan

1. Ummona ka Anumpa hut ahanta mut, Anumpa hut Chihowa ya ai iba chuvfa tok: Mihmut Anumpa hash ot Chihowa ya tok.

chitokaka
okchalinchi
chisus
hesaketvmese
jesus
wakanta yeshua
theword
word
apa
wakonda
dawkee
cesvsmekko
jenani
cesvs
niwaruhu
jeswah
daukei
ihilombishholitopa

CHEROKEE Lord's Prayer

Ogidoda, galvladi hehi, Galvquodiyu gesesdi
detsadovi. Tsagvwiyuhi gesv wiganvnugoi. Ani
elohi winigalisda hadanvtisgoi, nasgiya galvladi
tsinigalisdiha. Nidadodaquisv ogalisdayedi sgivsi
gohi iga. Digesgivsiquono desgidugvi, nasgiya
tsidigayotsineho tsotsidugi. Ale tlesdi
Udagoliyediyi gesv, widisgiyatinvstanvgi,
sgiyudalesgesdiquosgini, Uyo gesvi.
Tsatseligayeno tsagvwiyuhi gesvi, ale
Tsalinigidiyi gesvi, ale Etsalvquodiyu nigohilvi.
Emenv.

CHOCTAW Lord's Prayer

Piki vba ish binili ma, chi hohchifo hvt holitopashki. Ish apehlichika vlashke. Nana ish ai ahni ka yakni pakna ya a yohmi kvt, vba yakni a yohomi mak O chiuhmashke. Himak nitak ihlpak pim ai vlhpesa kako ish pi ipetashke. Mikmvt Nana il aheka puta ish pi

Kashofi kvt, pishno vt nana pim aheka puta il i kashofi chatuk a ish chiyuhmichashke. Mikmut anukpvlika yoka ik ia chik pim aiahno hosh, amba nan-isht-aiahli pi a hlakofihinchaske: Apehlichika, mikmvt nan-isht-aiahli, micha isht aholitopa aiena kvt chimmi a bilia yoke. Amen.

HYMNS

1. *Tribal hymns*
2. *Muscogee when Christians arrive*
3. *Cherokee blessed be the Tie*
4. *Comanche 54 Who is listening to our Master Jesus Calling?*
5. *Cherokee I will tell what God has done for me*
6. *Osage call on him*
7. *At the cross Cherokee Choctaw Muscogee*
8. *Amazing Grace Caddo Cherokee Cheyenne*
9. *Amazing Grace Choctaw Kiowa Muscogee Potawatomi*
10. *Potawatomi Amazing Grace*
11. *Caddo come and go to that land*
12. *Ponca Wakonda tha-ho da nee Kiowa Daw-kee dahay*
13. *Pawnee Sic see wey ta tee tah   Kiowa Ah-ho Dau-kei*
14. *Comanche 77 We will work until Jesus comes*
15. *Cherokee guide me, Jehovah*
16. *Muscogee it could be the very end*
17. *Cherokee Heaven beautiful*
18. *Osage have faith in God*
19. *Muscogee beautiful land*
20. *Comanche 62 Jesus is coming*
21. *Cherokee Christ Second Coming*
22. *Kiowa 29 The Son of God is with you be happy*
23. *Cherokee just as I am*
24. *Kiowa Dau Kgeh E Thinsa Pbah*
25. *Cherokee one drop of blood*
26. *Cheyenne Cherokee orphan child*
27. *Muscogee Estvmvn Follvtskis*
28. *Comanche 12 I prayed to God*
29. *Cherokee Jesus my all*
30. *Euchee He-lay I go no Choctaw 55 Christian hope*

31. *Muscogee Mekusapiket Yicof*

32. *Osage Jesus Take Me far away*

33. *Choctaw 21*

34. *Kiowa you who are going along God's way*

35. *Comanche 16 Someone has made a way for you*

36. *Choctaw 48 Choctaw 138 The Gospel*

37. *Cherokee Rock of Ages*

38. *Choctaw Sweet by and by*

39. *Muscogee Sweet by and by*

40. *Choctaw 112   Choctaw 35*

41. *Kiowa the son of God*

42. *Muscogee My peace I leave with you*

43. *Choctaw 11*

44. *Muscogee Cehotosakvtes Cenaorakvtes*

45. *Choctaw 120 Judgment*

46. *Muscogee Jesus Mico*

47. *Comanche Jesus tsa-tsu   Muscogee Heleluyvn*

48. *Muscogee Hvlwen Heckvyofyn*

49. *Muscogee Jesus Polthkelay Kahn*

50. *Choctaw 53 give me Christ or else I die*

51. *Muscogee pray for me*

52. *Kiowa Prayer song*

53. *Kiowa keep on praying to him*

54. *Muscogee Joy to the World*

55. *Muscogee Lord dismiss us*

1

TRIBAL HYMNS

MUSCOGEE (CREEK) WHEN CHRISTIANS ARRIVE

Me-ko-sah-pul-ket yeh-chof ah-kah-wap-keta net-tun.

Cesus hulwe lai-kan ah-kah-wap-kah-kah-thes.

Eth-ke-nah-kul-ke yeh-chof ah-kah-wap-keta net-tun. Cesus hulwe lai-kan ah-kah-wap-kah-kah-thes.

Po-tha-hul-ke yeh-chof ah-kah-wap-keta net-tun.

Cesus hulwe lai-kan ah-kah-wap-kah-kah-thes.

Po-cha-sul-ke yeh-chof ah-kah-wap-keta net-tun. Cesus hulwe lai-kan ah-kah-wap-kah-kah-thes.

Po-wun-tah-ke yeh-chof ah-kah-wap-keta net-tun. Cesus hulwe lai-kan ah-kah-wap-kah-kah-thes.

Ho-pue-tah-ke yeh-chof ah-kah-wap-keta net-tun. Cesus hulwe lai-kan ah-kah-wap-kah-kah-thes.

CHEROKEE BLEST BE THE TIE

Doe heed ah guy yoo hee

Noe hee dey dah tloe hee Gah luh lah dee oo wha suh hee

Clah yeh dah goe hee jee

Wee dey doe hey sdee quo Ee ghee doe dah wee gah ney luh Gah luh lah dee joe suh.

COMANCHE

Hymn #54
Composed by (Mrs. Emmett Cox —
Namahkuu)

Introduction

Hakaru tahu Narumi?a Jesasi Pumu
nimaihkana nakawunuuyu.

(Who is listening to our Master Jesus
calling?)

(Repeat Introduction)
|kuhu sokoba?a pu numihpe suabema pu
narahwuna wunuhpe.

(Here on earth He was nailed to the cross.)

Tahi sumunarumakaku?i.
(He paid for all of us.)

Suruse suni?yutu,
(That's the reason,)

Tahu numunaina tahi makwitso?aikutu?i,
(He is going to save us all,)

Tahi sumubetsuuyu.

CHEROKEE I WILL TELL WHAT GOD HAS DONE FOR ME

Ah nee yoe ee jee loo gi eyjah good yuh duh

Nee gah duh ee jah duh dah sdey stee

Dahjah no hey hey lee noo lee hey lee s'duh ee, Ah yuhjee sah ah ghee doe lee juh:

Dahjuh noe (Hey hey lee)

Noo lee hey (Lee sduh ee)

Ah yah jee sah ah ghee doe lee juh (ahjuh)

Gah luh lah dee ey hee jee sgah nuh sey luh ghee: Joo yoe tluh wee gah nuh noo goe guh,

Ah yah noo lee ah qua dey doe wah dee suh ghee, Goe hoo stee nee jee nah yeh sguh nah.

OSAGE

by T. Redcorn

    Ki-pa Tha O

Wa-ka^n-ta zhin-ke

Ki-pa Tha O (ya ho way)

Wi-a^n-kshe a-the, O

A-hu (ai-yo, ya ho way)

    Ni Wasuhu (ya ho way)

Ki-pa Tha O (ya ho way)

Wi-a^n-kshe the (ya ho way)

O-wi-ki-a, O

Wi-a^n-kshe a the, O

A-hu (ai-yo, ya ho way)

(Call on him, Jesus, Call on him. I tell you the truth as I tell you this, I tell you the truth, He'll Come. Holy Spirit, Call on him. I tell you the truth as I tell you this, I tell you the truth, He'll Come.

"AT THE CROSS"

Alas and did my Savior bleed and did my Sovereign die? Would he devote that sacred head for sinners such as I?

At the cross, at the cross, where I first saw the light And the burden of my heart rolled away; It was there by faith I received my sight And now I am happy all the day

CHEROKEE

Oo ney thla nuh hee oo wey jee

Eegah gwo yuh hey ee

Hnah quo joe suh wee oo loe sey Ee gah gwoo yuh hoe null.

CHOCTAW

Shilombish holitopa ma!

Ish minti pulla cha

Hatak ilbusha pia ha Ish pi yukpalashke.

MUSCOGEE (CREEK)

Aie ha! Kut! Cha he-sa-yeech-ka Chata pu-lat-kut haks?

Moh-men um mekko e-lut haks? Chun-ta yo-mus-i-yan.

AMAZING GRACE

   CADDO

Dah-newn bah-'we-aht, Ah-ah ha-you

He-E-k'ay is-dud, dah-ah

Se tah-yah o-e-ah

Ha-bah-lah ku-bay-yah

Nah-dah-new tah chay-bah.

   CHEROKEE

Oo neh thlah nuh hee Oo weh jee

Ee gah goo yuh heh ee

Hnah qwo jo suh Wee oo loh seh

Ee gah goo yuh ho nuh

   CHEYENNE

Jesus ne-ta wo-we ho-ni

Say-yo key-ya m-yo-tigh

Say-yo kay-wo-wo-ni

She-hi tsoy-she

Aho ne-ta hay-tone

CHOCTAW

Shilombish Holitopa ma!

Ish minti pulla cha,

Hatak ilbusha pia ha

Ish pi yukpalashke.

KIOWA

Daw-k'ee dahay dawtsahy hee tsow'ah

Daw-k'ee dahay dawtsahy hee.

Bay dawtsahay-taw, gaw aym owthah t'aw.

Daw-k'ee dahay dawysahy h'ee.

MUSCOGEE (Creek)

Pu-yah-fek-cha He-that ut-et,

Vn-en uh-cha pa-kus

Cha fe-ke o-vun un lai-kus,

Um oh-ha-tah-lai-yus

POTAWATOMI

Noshk shehm-nit-to kee zhuh-when-mah,

Gwis-sahn kee meen-go-nahn;

Kee mee-when-mahn ah-tee-mahk-see-yahn,

Kos-nahn k'tah-ban-go-nahn

POTAWATOMI Amazing Grace

Noshk shehm-nit-to kee zhuh-when-mah,

Gwis-sahn kee meen-go-nahn;

Kee mee-when-mahn ah-tee-mahk-see-yahn,

Kos-nahn k'tah-ban-go-nahn

Kshehm-nit-to gwis-sahn ge yah-wah,

Shah-zhos kee zhin-kah-sot.

Hehsh-pah-nah ween keem mnozh-jit-shkaht

Ah-wee ko-sahb-mee-meht

Meeg-wahtch-to-nahn ah-zhwan-mish-nok

Ah-jah tah-mahk-see-yahk

Knob-maht-so-when mee-nah meesh-ko-swen

K'tah-meen-goy-go jeh-yak.

CADDO Come and Go to That Land (With exception of Chorus repeat each verse three times.)

(1)Ke-wht ha-U nah-tse de-sah

Nah Ah-ah Nah Ah-ah

(2) Ke-wht ha-U nah-tse de-sah

Nah Ah-ah

(1) Hay sah-yah ko-tse de-sah

Nah Ah-ah Nah Ah-ah

(2) Hay sah-yah ko-tse de-sah

Nah Ah-ah

(1) Ha-ah-hutt knh-hay-ah

Nah Ah-ah Nah Ah-ah

(2) Ha-ah-hutt knh-hay-ah

Nah Ah-ah

(1) Ha-ah-hutt khn-oos sin-nah

Nah Ah-ah Nah Ah-ah

(2) Ha-ah-hutt khn-oos sin-nah

Nah Ah-ah

PONCA

Wa konda tha-ho da nee

Wa konda tha-ho da nee gah

We-blah-ha mah-blee

Wa konda tha-ho da nee

Wa konda tha-ho da nee

Wa konda tha-ho da nee

Wa konda tha-ho da nee

Wa konda tha-ho da nee gah we-blah-ha
mah-blee

KIOWA

Daw-k'ee dahay dawtsahy hee tsow'ah

Daw-k'ee dahay dawtsahy hee.

Bay dawtsahy-taw, gaw aym owthah t'aw.

Daw-k'ee dahay dawysahy h'ee.

PAWNEE

Sic see wey ta tee tah
Sic see wey ta tee tah

*A te us ee dee ah ha ke tah coo,
Sic see wey ta tee tah
Sic see wey ta tee tah
(repeat from *)

KIOWA

Ah-ho Dau-kei yahn tai ohm mai
Ah-ho Dau-kei yahn tai ohm mai
Dau-chai pado yahn tai ohm mai
Dau-chai pado yahn tai ohm mai
Geah tape kom na yahn tai ohm mai
Mah ohm dai.

COMANCHE 77

Composed by Pete Coffee

Jesus ha pitu?ipetu tanu Urii turu?ai miaru?i,
(We'll work until Jesus comes,)

Urii turu?ai miaru?i.
(We'll keep on working.)

Chorus
Okuro Tomoba?atu,
(Up in Heaven,)

Tamu uruu ninusupetipu katu tanu, urii turu?
ai miaru?i.

(He has promised us a place, we'll keep on
working.)

Urii turu?ai miaru?i,
(We'll keep on working,)

Tamu uruu sutaikatu tanu urii turu?ai
miaru?i.
(He has blessed us, we'll keep on working.)

(Repeat Chorus)

CHEROKEE Guide Me, Jehovah

Squa tee ne she stee ye how wah,

El lah deh gah ee suh ee,

Jee wah nah gah lee you ah yuh,

Jah lee nee gee dee nee hee.

    Nee goe heel uh,

    Skee stey lee sgey stee yoe goe,

    Nee goe hee luh,

    Skee stey lee sgey stee yoe goe.

Nuh woe tee gah luh goe guh ee

Ah nuh woe skee stoo ee see,

Ah jee luh noe oo loe ghee luh,

Ee guh ee ah ee sey stee.

    Skee stey lee skee

    Dee skee gah hnah wah dee dah

    Skee stey lee skee

    Dee skee gah hnah wah dee dah

MUSCOGEE (CREEK)

ESPOKETIS OMES KERRESKOS

Ees-poh-kei-tes Omes Keth-thes-kos

(It could be the very end, we may not know)

Ees-poh-kei-tes Omes Keth-thes-kos

Ees-poh-kei-tes Omes Keth-thes-kos

O-ho-pul-tah-ke ah-pei-yun-nah

Ees-poh-kei-tes Omes Keth-thes-kos

Ees-poh-kei-tes Omes Keth-thes-kos

Poh-tha-hul-kee ah-pei-yun-nah

Ees-poh-kei-tes Omes Keth-thes-kos

Ees-poh-kei-tes Omes Keth-thes-kos

Uh-kuh-sum-ulke ah-pei-yun-nah

Ees-poh-kei-tes Omes Keth-thes-kos

Ees-poh-kei-tes Omes Keth-thes-kos

CHEROKEE Heaven Beautiful #36

Oo nay la nv nee, oo way jee nee gah dee,

Ay dee gay you he nah quo dee dah lay hv,

Woo low sv ee dah ee say stee dee gah dah,

Ne yv say stee no de gah dah gay you hee.

    Gah lah low (gah lah low)

    You woe do (you woe do)

    Nah nee way (nah nee way)

    Yee hoe wah (yee hoe wah)

    Jew jee lee (jew jee lee)

    Ah skah nee (ah skah nee)

    Nooy ha nah (nooy ha nah)

    Joe, sv yee (joe, sv yee)

Oh guh wee you hee oo jay lee day dee gah,

Nah wah de say stee, ah nee eh low geh suh

Sah quo no new stee, dee say stee je sah gah,

Low nay, dv nah skee, day gah ee, nee say stee.

OSAGE

by T. Redcorn

Wa-ka^n-ta I-ki-na^n-zhi

Ki-thi-su ta pa, i-ki-na^n-zhi

Pa-na ta aha, i-ki-na^n-zhi

i-ki-na^n-zhi i-ki-na^n-zhi

(Have Faith in God, and in the end, he will remember you..)

MUSCOGEE (CREEK) Beautiful Land

Ekvna hearten

Ekvna hearten

Omo' momis komet vwatsken

Cesvs likan vpeyakvres

Erkenakv toyatskat

Erkenakv toyatskat

Omo' momis komet vwatsken

Cesvs likan vpeyakvres

Purahvlke toyatskat

Purahvlke toyatskat

Omo' momis komet vwatsken

Cesvs likan vpeyakvres

COMANCHE 62

Composed by Dorothy Komahcheet

Jesus tsa tsu tahi tsometu?i,
Unuha naboohkahutu?i.

(Jesus is coming, are you ready?)

Chorus

Tahi naboohkaku, tahi tso?metu?i.

(Are you ready, He will pick us up.)

Okuho tomoba?atu tahi tso?metu?i, Unuha
naboohka.

(He's going to take us to Heaven, are you
ready?)

Tahi naboohkaku, tahi tso?metu?i,
okuho tomoba?atu.

(When we're ready, He will pick us up,
and take us to Heaven.)

(Repeat Chorus)

CHEROKEE Christ's Second Coming #87

Oo neh thlah nuh hee Oo weh jee

Ee gah goo yuh heh ee

Hnah qwo jo suh Wee oo loh seh

Ee gah goo yuh ho nuh

  Oo jah tee yoo wo doo nah nee wey nah nah nee

  Ee gah do juh loo sah doo jo suh yee

  Gey nah nee wee gah nah nah noo go goo

 Joo wah doe hee do dee dah ne loo.

Ee seh no Ee oo neh jeh ee

Ah yoo no Doo leh nuh,

Tah lee neh Duh jee loo jee lee

Oo duh neh Oo neh juh

KIOWA #29 THE SON OF GOD IS WITH YOU,
BE HAPPY

Daw-k' yah-ee gaw-thahy-dow,
aym-owthat-dawpay.

Daw-k' yah-ee gaw-thahy-dow,
gaw-thahy-dow,

Aym-ow-dawpay gaw-thahy-dow-dow.

Daw-k' yah-ee gaw-thahy-dow,
aym-owthat-dawpay.

Daw-k' yah-ee gaw-thahy-dow,
gaw-thahy-dow,

Aym-ow-dawpay gaw-thahy-dow-dow.

Daw-k' yah-ee gaw-thahy-dow
Aym-owthah-dawpay.

CHEROKEE-JUST AS I AM

Nah qua sduh quo, gah jee ska nee

Jah ghee guh sgah qua sdo duh

Ah lee skee yah nee skuhjee sah

Wee guh lee jee, wee guh loo jee.

Nah qua sduh quo skee skey lee skee

Nee jee gah tee dee sduh nah noe Jee sgah
nuh ah gee huh sgee yee

Wee guh 1oo jee, wee guh loo jee.

Nah quo skuh quo ah jee yoe ee

Guh nee duh ah qua oo lee sguh

Ah ley nee gah uh quo jee sah

Wee guh loo jee, wee guh loo jee.

KIOWA

Dau Kgeh E Thinsa Pbah

Dau Kgeh E Thinsa Pbah aum pbay doe ha

Dau Kgeh E Thay doe kee bone ma ba ahn

Jesus aham pbay doe thinsa pbah haim;

Hate they bay Dau chi ee

Thay bay doe chi ee

Thay bay doe chi ee

Thay bay doe chi ee gah ohn

Dau kgeh pbay doe kee gah ohn

Dau kgeh pbay doe kee gah ohn

Dau kgeh ee thinsa pbah aum pbah doe haim.

CHEROKEE One Drop of Blood

Gah do dah juh yah Duh neh lee Jee sah

O gah jeh lee Jah guh wee yoo hee

O gah lee gah lee Yuh hah qwo yeh no

Jo gee luh wee sdah neh dee yee.

O gah jeh lee gah (o gah jeh lee gah)

Jah guh wee yoo hee (jah guh wee yoo hee)

Jah jeh lee gah no (jah jeh lee gah no)

Jah guh wee yoo hee (jah guh wee yoo hee)

O gah jeh lee gah (O gah je lee ga)

Jah guh wee yoo hee (Jah guh wee yoo hee)

Jah jeh ee lee gah (jah jeh ee lee gah)

Jah guh wee yoo hee (jah guh wee yoo hee)

CHEYENNE

Ah ha O ha O mesh I vot zi so he ye

Ah ha ha ay

E ya ha O na ot zi yo tsi so ah ha ha ay

E ya ha O

CHEROKEE Orphan Child

U we dolisdi kanegv gatv gia tsisa

Unido dana nunehvna una daniyvdv

    Diniyotli Aniyotli Galvadi Tstinuga

    Diniyotli Aniyotli Galvadi Tstinuga

    Diniyotli Aniyotli Galvadi Tstinuga

    Tsunodu he wane hesdi Galvladi

Tsagvwi yu hi naquu tatbuga ditsenvsv

Tsunoye niquu dehi niyvsesadi nigohilv

MUSCOGEE (CREEK) Estvmvn Follvtskis

Estvmvn Estomen Follvtskis

Vmemekosvpvcken Aneu

    Ceme Mekosvpvkin.

Erkenvkvlke Toyvtskvt,

Momis Komvkes,

Estvmvn Estomen Follvtskis

Vmemekosvpvcken Aneu

    Ceme Mekosvpvkin.

Mekosvpvlke Toyvtskvt, etc.

Cvrvhvlke Toyvtskvt, etc

Cvcusvlke Toyvtskvt, etc

Cvwvntvke Toyvtskvt, etc

Hopuetvke Toyvtskvt, etc

COMANCHE12

By George Kaudawthy (Khyooy-ay-daw-daw)

Daw-k'ee gyah-dawtsahy naw ay-paygyah-
owthah-awmay, ah-owthah-daw dow.
Daw-k'ee gyah-dawtsahy naw Ay-paygyah-
owthah-awmay, ah-owthah-daw,
ah-owthah-daw, ah-owthah-daw dow.
Daw-k'ee gyah-dawtsahy naw Ay-paygyah-
owthah-awmay, ah-owthah-daw dow.

(I prayed to God and He gladdens my spirit, I
am glad. I prayed to God and He gladdens my
spirit, I am glad, I am glad, I am glad. I
prayed to God and He gladdens my spirit, I
am glad.)

CHEROKEE- JESUS MY ALL

Oo ney thla nuh hee oo wey ee

Joe suh ee hnah quo woo loe suh

Jee yah lee sgah sdoe dee nah sgee

Woo loe suh wuh dahjee loe see.

    Ah yah doe lee wee gah nuh nuh

    Oo nah dah tee woo nee loe suh

    Oo ney thla nuh hee joo woe luh

    Hnah quo ah sey wee jee gah tee.

Goe hee ghee guh quah ley ney duh

Gah dah tee squo gah luh lah dee Jee yah
dah doe lee sdah ney hoe Ah sey no jee yah
tloe goe quo.

EUCHEE

He-lay I go no, He-lay on fay no. (2)

San-na chee any ai yo on,

Na ya hay lay sak ah ya no.

Cho-way nan a ah yoan

Na ya hay lay sak ah ya no

Cho-da da nay ah yoan,

Na ya hay lay sak ah ya no

De-ah tee tee nay ah yoan,

Na ya hay lay sak ah ya no

CHOCTAW Christians hope #55

   Uh-bah me-ko-pullah kah

Im uhl-lah huh-che-ah mah!

Tah-lo-ah ho-le-to-pah

Huhsh tahloah pullahshke

    Huhsh tah-lo-ho-wah ho-kuht

Che-suhs huh-che ho-hu-hlo,

Huhche okchahlinche ka,

Huhsh im ahnahyahchashke.

CREEK (MUSCOGEE) Mekusaplket Yicof

Mekusapvlket yicof akvwpketa nettvn.
Cesvs Hvlwe likan akvwvpkakvres.

Estenvlke yicof akvwpketa nettvn.
Cesvs Hvlwe likan akvwvpkakvres.

Porahvlke yicof akvwpketa nettvn.
Cesvs Hvlwe likan akvwvpkakvres.

Pocuslike yicof akvwpketa nettvn.
Cesvs Hvlwe likan akvwvpkakvres.

Powantake yicof akvwpketa nettvn.
Cesvs Hvlwe likan akvwvpkakvres.

Hopuetake yicof akvwpketa nettvn.
Cesvs Hvlwe likan akvwvpkakvres.

OSAGE

by T. Redcorn

Jesus a^n-tha-lu-za we-hi-tse (4 times)

(Jesus take me far away)

O we-hi-tse

(far away)

Ma-xe man-shi-ta the-tse (yo-oh) we-hi-tse

(To heave, there, far away)

Wa-nan-xe wi-ta a-lu-za we-hi-tse (2 times)

(my spirit, take it far away)

O we-hi-tse

(far away)

Wa-nan-xe wi-ta the-tse (yo-oh) we-hi-tse.

(my spirit, take it far away)

CHOCTAW #21

Uba pin Chitokaka yut,

Oh Ile kostinichi.

Et pim ahanchi pulla ka

Eho haklo pullashke.

    Hatak yoshoba pia hut

    Pin Chisus achukma ka

    il I nukkilla hinla cho?

    Anukfilit ke pisa.

Yoshoba bieka hocha

Aiokpuloka fehna

E chukowa hosi hona,

Pi nukhaklo tok oke.

KIOWA YOU WHO ARE GOING ALONG GOD'S WAY, BE HAPPY

Daw-k'yah-aym aym-ah-day aym-ow-dawpay.

Jeezahy how'awn-thahy aym-ah---day aym-ow-dawpay.

K'yahkowndah gaw-aw---taw ah-naw ah-kheebow-taw.

Jeezahy how'awn-thahy gyah-ow.

(You are going along God's way, be happy. You who are going on Jesus' road, be happy. He will give you life and you will be saved. On Jesus' road there's joy.)

COMANCHE 16

Hawnday gyaht-thayn-ts'ow awmay-day. ;
Daw-k'yah-ee daw gaw gyaht-thayn-ts'ow
awmay,

Awgaw hawnday gyaht-thayn-ts'ow
awmay-day.
Daw-k'yah-ee daw gaw gyaht-thayn-ts'ow
awmay,
gaw owday gyaht-thayn-ts'ow awmay-day.
Ah-dawtsahy-hee-taw-day.

(Someone has made a way for you. It is the
Son of God and He made a way for you, The
One that made a way for you. It is the Son of
God and He made a way for you, and in
gladness He made.)

CHOCTAW #48

Shilombish Holitopa ma!

Ish minti pulla cha,

Hatak ilbusha pia ha

Ish pi yukpalashke.

Pi chukush nus atukma

Ant ish okchulashke,

Ish pi yohbiechikbano;

E chim aiahnishke.

CHOCTAW The Gospel #138

Aiokchaya anumpa hosh Ay aka, ho haklo:

Yoshubut ilbusha puta Isht kostini yoke.

Ayoshoba a kvnivt Aiokhilika yo.

Il itvnowa hoh kia Isht pi kuchi yoke.

Aiokcyaya yoke yakni Moma fullota kvt I ik
achi;

vba ai okla't achi mak inlashke.

CHEROKEE ROCK OF AGES

Jee sah jah lee nee ghee duh

Dee squad ah nee luh ghee quo

Ah ley gah luh quo dee yoo

Jah juh nuh hee jah ghee guh

Sgee nuh gah luh dah hnah quo

Ah ley ah sey sgee sdey luh.

Ee you noe nee goe hee luh

Ah ma dee jee gah doe lee

Yee dey gah ah ley nah squo

Oh sduh yee nee gah duh ney

Nee gah duh ah sey quo quo

See quo jee sgah nah yee ghee.

Nee hee sgee nee juh suh hee

Jee sah gey skee sdey luh dee

Nee hee jah yoe hoo suh ee

Gah lee sgah sdoe dee sguh ee Jee loo ghee
dey jee nee yuh Gey dun eyjah duh nuh ee.

CHOCTAW Sweet by and by

Yakni Shoh pa ka-li achukma,

Yimmi ka pulla ho pisali;

Chisas at yammak o ahanta,

At asha pim ibit ia tok.

    Kanimash inli ho

    Il-itta fama chi hakinli.

Ont at ish ai yopikma enchil,

Im ilh-talowak talohonwat,

Pish shilombish nukhaklo tok kia

Na yuk-pa bieka he yoke.

MUSCOGEE (CREEK) Sweet by and by

Ekvnv herusat ocet os,

Nette sen hvyayvket omes

Vkvsvmkv eteropotten

Hopvyis, heceye tetayes.

       Oketv cumpusan

       Mv tvpaiv mimv herusan,

       Oketv cumpusan

       Mv tvpalvn teheceyvres.

Afvchakat en yvhiketvn

Mvtvpalvn yvhikeyvres;

Stofis pu fehnokhokekares;

Yuksv-sekon fekapeyvres.

CHOCTAW Meditation on Death #112

Nitak kanima fehna ho.

Si ai illi hokma,

Aki uba binili mu

Is sa halanlashke.

Chisus pulla tuk mak oma,

Si ai illi hokmut,

Uba yakni achukma ka

Oma la hi oke.

CHOCTAW #35

Chisus pulla kuto

Pi nukhaklo hocha,

Iki Chihowa issa cha,

Minti ula hatok.

Yakni lusa hoka

Ant ahanta hokut

Okla ilbusha pisa mut,

Nukhaklo tok oke.

KIOWA DAW-K'YAH-EE TAYYSAY-PAH AHM PAYDOW HAYM

The Son of God on the Cross Died Because of You

Daw-k'yah-ee tahysay-pah ahm paydow haym,

Daw-k'yah-ee tay daw-kheebown-maw,
bah-ah.

Jeezahaah ahm paydow tahysaw-pah---haym.

Hay---t tay bay-dawtsahy-hee

Tay bay-dawtsahy-hee, tay bay-dawtsahy-hee,

tay bay-dawtsahy-hee gyah-ow.

Daw-k'yah paydow kheedah ow,

Daw-k' yah paydow kheedah ow,

Daw-k'yah-ee tahysaw-paw ahm paydow
haym.

(The Son of God on the cross died because
of you. The Son of God is going to save us
all, come on. Jesus because of you died on
the cross. Let all of us keep praying on. All
of us keep praying on, all of us keep praying
on, all of us keep praying on as there's joy in
it. Because of God each day is joyful,
because of God each day is joyful, the Son of
God on the cross died because of you.)

MUSCOGEE (Creek) My Peace I Leave With You

"Vn herketvn cem wikvkis,

Ekvnv es temat onkon;

Ce feken penkvlehcaskvs:"

Cesvs kicet 'momayvtes.

"Ayiyvtet rvlakayof,

Cvnanken ce hayvkares;

Momen estvn likiyate,

Cemeu mvn vpokvgskves."

"Holayeckv apvkeko

Afvcketvt cem ocvkes;

Holwayeckv vkerrickv

Orve seko tvlofvn.

CHOCTAW #11

Hatak hush puta ma Ho ho minti
Hatak hush puta ma Ho ho minti
Hatak hush puta ma
Yakni achukma kat
Uba talaiushke
Ho ho minti.
Hatak hush moma ma Ho ho yimmi
Hatak hush moma ma Ho ho yimmi
Hatak hush moma ma
Chisus im anumpa
Hush yimmi pullashke
Ho ho yimmi.

MUSCOGEE (Creek) Cehotosvkes

Cehotosakvtes Cenaorakvtes

Momis komet awatcken oh apey akares
hvlwen.

Mekosapvlk' apeyanna,

ayetan ceyaceko!

Momis komet awatcken oh apey akares
hvlwen.

Erkenvkv apeyanna, ayetan ceyaceko!

Momis komet awatcken oh apey akares
hvlwen.

Cehotosakvtes Cenaorakvtes

Momis komet awatcken oh apey akares
hvlwen.

CHOCTAW Judgement #120

Ne-tahk ish-tah-e-yo-pik-muh-no,

Che-suhs uht me-hen-the,

"Uhm uhl ah-ho-le-to-pah mah!

Che hoht ah-yah lish-ke

    Ah hohl-lo, Ah hohl-lo,

    Ah hohl-lo fee-nah-shkee.

    Si ulth-to-buht pee-ah-huht

    Ah hohl-lo fee-nah-shkee

"Chem ah-yah-shah ik-be le-hosh

E-yah le tok-o-chah

Chem ah-tah-yah-le tok-osh

Che hoht uhl-ah lish-ke

MUSCOGEE (Creek) Cesvs Mekko

Cesvs Mekko Hvlwen likes Hvlwe tvlofv min.

Cesvs Mekko Hvlwen likes Hvlwe tvlofv min.

Mekosapvlke apeyanna Hvlwe tvlofv min.

Mekosapvlke apeyannaHvlwe tvlofv min.

Porahvlke apeyanna Hvlwe tvlofv min.

Porahvlke apeyannaHvlwe tvlofv min.

Pocusvlke apeyanna Hvlwe tvlofv min.

Pocusvlke apeyanna Hvlwe tvlofv min.

Powantake apeyanna Hvlwe tvlofv min.

Powantake apeyanna Hvlwe tvlofv min.

Hopuetake apeyanna Hvlwe tvlofv min.

Hopuetake apeyanna Hvlwe tvlofv min.

COMANCHE

God-ta poe-e-tsa d'a-ve-tse tsa ta-oh-tue me-ah na d'a

Go-ta poe-e-tsa d'a-ve-tse ta-oh-tue me-ah na ta-vis-ko

Jesus tsa-tsu su-me yeh-kwe-tah na-voy-tsa tsa-ta-oh-tue me-ah na d'a.

MUSCOGEE (Creek) Heleluyvn

Heleluyvn yahakakees, Hele-Heleluyvn.

Heleluyvn yahakakees, Hele-Heleluyvn.

Mekosapulket minvn vpokes,

Hele-Heleluyvn.

Elthkenahkahlket minvn vpokes,

Hele-Heleluyvn

Pucusvlket minvn vpokes,

Hele-Heleluyvn

Hopuetaket minvn vpokes,

Hele-Heleluyvn

Vksamvlke minvn vpokes,

Hele-Heleluyvn

MUSCOGEE (Creek) Hvlwen Heckvyofyn

Hvlwen Heckvyofyn,

Hvlwen Heckvyofyn,

Hvlwen Heckvyofyn, Hesvketvmese.

Mekosapv Mekosvpvks

Mekosapv Ayemvhs

Hvlwe Tvlofvminvn.

Hopeetake Mekosvpvks

Hopetake Ayemvhs

Hvlwe Tvlofvminvn.

Puwantake Mekosvpvks

Pwantake Ayemvhs

Hvlwe Tvlofvminvn.

Vkvsamvlke Mekosvpvks

Vkvsamvlke Ayemvhs

Hvlwe Tvlofvminvn.

MUSCOGEE (Creek) Jesus Polthkelay Kahn

Jesus Polthkelay Kahn

Jesus Polthkelay Kahn

Jesus Polthkelay Kahn

Mun te-he cha kah thles.

Mekosahpulke ah peyan non

Mekosahpulke ah peyan non

Mekosahpulke ah peyan non

Mun te-he cha kah thles.

Pomahpultahke ah peyan non

Pomahpultahke ah peyan non

Pomahpultahke ah peyan non

Mun te-he cha kah thles.

Ethkenahkahlke ah peyan non

Ethkenahkahlke ah peyan non

Ethkenahkahlke ah peyan non

Mun te-he cha kah thles.

CHOCTAW 53. "Give Me Christ, or else I Die,"

Chitokaka ma! chi haksobish a
Et welit, chin tahpahanla li ka
Auet is sa haklo cha, nana ka
Chim asihilhha li ka et Umà;
    Klaist a auet is sum ihissashke;
    Keyukmuno, sulla he banoshke.
 Täli holliso, micha nanasi
Yakni 'luppa asha, yohmi kuno
Is sumakbano, chi ahni la wa;
Klaist ak bano, ho sa bahannushke
    Klaist a auet is sum ihissashke;
    Keyukmuno, sulla he banoshke.

MUSCOGEE (CREEK) PRAY FOR ME

Es-tuh-mun es-to-men ful-latch-kes

a-me-me-ko-sah-patch-keen

Uh-neo, chem-me-me-ko-sah-pah-hes.

Eth-ke-nah-gul-ge toi-yats-kat momes
komuh-kes.

Me-ko-sah-pul-ke toi-yats-kat momes
komuh-kes.

Po-mah-pul-tah-ke toi-yats-kat momes
komuh-kes.

Un-his-ses-ul-ge toi-yats-kat memes
komuh-kes.

KIOWA Prayer Song

    Daw-k' yah-ee, ah-dawtsahy-ahn,

Daw-k' yah-ee, ah-dawtsahy-ahn.

Ahm dow gyah-daw dow ahn,

Ah-tsahn dow gyaht-t' ah-awm.

    Daw-k' yah-ee, ah-dawtsahy-ahn,

Daw-k' yah-ee, ah-dawtsahy-ahn.

Ahm khee-dah-day, dow ahn,

Che me-koh-sah-pe-yuh-te

KIOWA SON OF GOD, KEEP ON PRAYING TO HIM

Daw-k'yah-ee bah-dawtsahy-hee,

Daw-k'yah-ee bah-dawtsahy-hee.

Mahday-k'yahkow-maw ay-tsaht-haydaytaw naw,

Bah-owthah-t'aw.

Pay-hay k' yahdowmdah gaw-aw-taw naw,

Aym-owthah-t' aw.

(Son ofGod, keep on praying to Him, Son of God, keep on praying to Him. Up there in the heavenly life He will open the door, And you all will be happy. Deathless life He will give to you and, You will be happy.)

MUSCOGEE (CREEK) JOY TO THE WORLD

   Ah-fuch-kah-ges He-sai-ye-jut alaks

Mek-kon ah-kuh-sum-aks

Je-fek-hung-it yah-hai-gus

Oh-mul-gut yah-hai-gus

Oh-mul-gut yah-hai-gus

Oh-mul-gut, oh-mul-gut yah-hai-gah-ges.

   Heth-kun no-wit e-guh-nun en-fai-yats,

Me-hen-wan he-tha-go-sat

E-tul-wan sen fuh-che-jit-ohs

Es-to-we-mah-uh-het

Es-to-we-mah-uh-het

Es-to-we es-to-oh-we-mah-het,
Uh-no-gech-kah.

MUSCOGEE (CREEK) LORD, DISMISS US

Che me-koh-sah-pe-yuh-te
Mo-moh-sen tem ah-wah-hes.

Chen heth-ke-tun poh-wath-lus
Moh-met se-poo-wa-hee-chus.

Moh-men yum-mah e-gun-nuh;
En kah-pah-kah-kai-yo-vut

Chen lai-ke-tun tho-thai-jet;
Fe-kai-pe-tun poh yah-ches.